BOOM SCIENCE

MATERIALS

Georgia Amson-Bradshaw

BOOM SCIENCE

MATERIALS

Georgia Amson-Bradshaw

PowerKiDS press

Published in 2020 by The Rosen Publishing Group, Inc.
29 East 21st Street, New York, NY 10010

Cataloging-in-Publication Data

Names: Amson-Bradshaw, Georgia.
Title: Materials / Georgia Amson-Bradshaw.
Description: New York : PowerKids Press, 2020. | Series: Boom science |
Includes glossary and index.
Identifiers: ISBN 9781725303775 (pbk.) | ISBN 9781725303799 (library
bound) | ISBN 9781725303782 (6pack)
Subjects: LCSH: Materials--Juvenile literature.
Classification: LCC TA403.2 A56 2020 | DDC 620--dc23

Series Editor: Georgia Amson-Bradshaw
Series Designer: Rocket Design (East Anglia) Ltd

Picture acknowledgements:
Shutterstock: Matyas Rehak 6b, Andrew Rybalko 7t, Dmitrii Kazitsyn 9tl, genjok
9tc, John Kasawa 9tr, Susan Schmitz 10c, cynoclub 10bl, windu 11br, Andrew
Rybalko 11t, 11tr, prapann 14t, Okssi 14bl, africanstuff 15t, Teguh Mujiono
15c, Eric Isselee 15b, Nuttapong 17tr, helena0105 17b, Perry Kay 20t, dymax
20c, Anneka 20b, Evgeny Karandaev 21b, senee sriyota 22, vovan 23t, Hayati
Kayhan 24, Roman Medvid 25t

Illustrations by Steve Evans 12, 13, 18, 19, 26, 27

All design elements from Shutterstock.

Manufactured in the United States of America

CPSIA Compliance Information: Batch CSPK19: For Further Information contact Rosen Publishing,
New York, New York at 1-800-237-9932.

Glossary words are shown in bold.

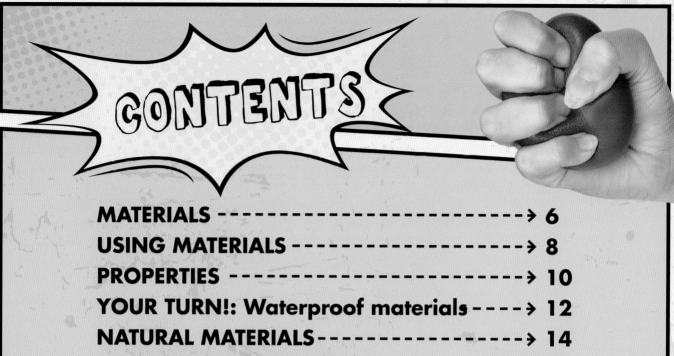

CONTENTS

MATERIALS

We make things from materials.

PAPER, COTTON, PLASTIC

There are many kinds of **materials**.
This book is made of **paper**. Your clothes
might be made of **cotton** or **plastic**.

WOW!

In Uyuni in Bolivia, some buildings are
made of salt! There is so much salt
in Uyuni that blocks of it can be cut
from the ground and used as bricks.